Embracing Your Super Power

Reactivating the Power of Imagination

By: Kevin D. Neal

Published by iCHAMPION Publishing

P.O. Box 2352 Frisco, TX 75034

Content edited by Dr. Nikia Hammonds-Blakely

Library of Congress Cataloging-in-Publication Data Publisher and Printing by iCHAMPION Publishing

Text Written By: Kevin D. Neal
Cover design by: iCHAMPION Publishing

EMBRACING YOUR SUPERPOWER
ISBN: 979-8-3732090-8-3

Categories:

Nonfiction > Self-Help > Creativity
Nonfiction > Self-Help > Motivational & Inspirational

Contents

Introduction 1

Chapter 1: Are You a Prisoner..2

Chapter 2: I Found It 5

Chapter 3: A Personal Triumph of Imagination 8

Chapter 4: Catch It Early...10

Chapter 5: To Know or Not to Know.....................................13

Chapter 6: Let's Talk Imagination..15

Chapter 7: What the World Needs Now 19

Chapter 8: How Do We Get There...24

Chapter 9: It's Time to Remember..28

Chapter 10: It's In Your Hands, Now What 31

Conclusion..34

References: 35

"Kevin Neal has given all of us a fine gift in his book, "Embracing Your SuperPower: Reactivating the Power of Imagination" He offers both challenge and encouragement in an inspirational and readable style. Kevin is a person of impeccable integrity and one whose own life and leadership embodies the vision he casts. In a world that desperately needs transformational changes, Kevin makes a strong case for nurturing and exercising imagination and then gives some practical guidance on how to do it. I recommend this volume with joy."

Dr. Daniel Vestal

Distinguished Professor of Baptist Leadership

Director of the Eula Mae and John Baugh Center for Baptist Leadership

Mercer University

Vestal_dg@Mercer.edu

Introduction

I believe that we are all born with a superpower that can overcome practically any obstacle, hurdle, or problem we face. It is a power that can envision and cannot be seen with physical eyes. It is a power that can see beyond what knowledge can show us. This power taps into a future that is incomprehensible by human standards. This power is the power of imagination. It is a power identified as faith in the religious sector, for what is faith but to see what cannot be seen with the human eye. But we often find ourselves in the prison of what we know, have known, can see, or have been told is true.

We often find it challenging to release things we've learned, concepts we have accepted for years, and beliefs we hold dear. As a matter of fact, there are certain ideals and knowledge that we cling to that we don't even know why we hold on to so tightly other than someone we trusted told us to. We attack or become highly defensive when that knowledge or ideal is challenged. It could be because we want to refrain from entertaining the thought that what we have accepted or believed to be true is no longer the standard or possibly because bit shines a light on the fact that we did not question this knowledge or ideology. Or it could be that we want to stay the same. Change is never easy. Heck, I still have some cassette tapes that it's hard for me to get rid of (don't laugh at me with your 8-track tapes 😊). But if we are to move forward and be everything we have been created to be, we must change! Escape the prison of the past, of antiquated thinking, of memories that do not serve you or help you to become your best self!

CHAPTER 1

Are You a Prisoner

"...in the wisdom of uncertainty lies the freedom from our past, from the known, which is the prison of past conditioning. And in our willingness to step into the unknown, the field of all possibilities, we surrender ourselves to the creative mind that orchestrates the dance of the universe."

—Deepak Chopra

There is a TV commercial where a man comes out and says, "Hi, I'm Dr. Rick, and I'm teaching these people not to become their parents." Have you ever seen that commercial? That's my favorite commercial. It is hilarious. It makes us laugh because we find so much truth in the depiction of the characters. Have you ever noticed yourself acting just like your parents? Saying some of the same things that you saw or heard your parents say when you were kids, which you thought were so lame or corny. As you get older, you find yourself doing or saying some of those lame, corny phrases or things. I have, and the older I get, the more those sayings and lame phrases come to mind.

I tell you this to say that I see myself becoming my dad in many ways. Whenever he encountered something that irritated him, he had a word that he would always use. That word was *Devilish.* Get that devilish dog! Pick up your devilish shoes! Turn those devilish lights out!

Now, every so often, when I get frustrated and can't find the right word to say, I find myself saying, *"that devilish thing."* (I knew I said I would never be that corny, but...)

We all are products of what we have seen, heard, and gone through. We store our life experiences, whether good or bad, in our memories. Memory is a good thing. - *It keeps us safe; it protects us...* Do you remember when you were a child, and you touched a hot stove or heater, and it burned you? Every time you go by a hot stove or heater now, your memory tells you, "don't touch that; it'll burn you."

*Jim Rohn once said, "*Treat the past as a school," meaning we should learn from our past from our memories. But I have learned throughout life *that our past and our memories can also be our prison*. It can keep us trapped from reaching out into the unknown, from dreaming, and soaring to unimaginable heights. Our memories can hold us hostage to what has happened in the past and keep us from envisioning what is possible for our present and future. Think about your past. Has anything happened to you that has made you defensive or cautious around others? Has a painful incident or situation caused you to isolate yourself? It is not the purpose of our memories or past to impede our growth or progress in life. We must learn to use our memories and past as a roadmap, not to stop moving forward but to know when to detour and avoid pitfalls.

If asked, most of us would say nothing holds us prisoner. We want to think that we make all our decisions because we have reasoned within our minds that "this is what I want to do." But is that really the truth? Are there places we refuse to go or people we refuse to come in contact with simply because of past experiences that evoke bad memories? Sometimes we may even drive 15 minutes out of our way, so we don't have to pass a particular place with bad memories.

We all have had bad memories and experiences in our past, but we must never allow them to hold us hostage. Own what happened. Own what was done or said to you, and then press forward. Yes, it will sting when you see that person, go past that place, or hear that song, but keep moving forward. The more you own it and face it, the less it will sting and the further you can go. The key is to see yourself going past that point (Imagination).

CHAPTER 2

I Found It

"Logic will get you from A to B. Imagination will take you everywhere."

—Albert Einstein

There's an old proverb that says, "curiosity killed the cat"...How many have heard that one? Well, my dad loved to use that proverb when we were kids. Whenever we would ask too many questions or try to investigate something that he didn't want us to, he would say, "all right now, curiosity killed the cat." That would always shut everything down. Not that we knew exactly what that meant, but hearing the words "killed" and "cat" was enough for us to stop in our tracks.

After I began to have children of my own (and started becoming my dad), often, my children would become overly inquisitive (as all children do) about something that I didn't want to reveal. My memory brought to my mind that same old proverb my dad used to quote. I said to my children, "all right, curiosity killed the cat." Thinking in my mind, "this would just shut it down like it did when we were kids." Wrong!

Then one of the kids said, "Daddy, how did curiosity kill the cat?"... I was like a deer in headlights. In what must have only been a few seconds, it felt like a lifetime had gone by.

Why didn't we ever think to ask my dad this question?!! Think, Think, Think...

I had Flashbacks from my military days... *(there I was.....* *surrounded by enemy fire, dive, dive,* **G**renade, fire-fire, low crawl!!!)* no, not really.

But finally, a light bulb went off*!!!* That's when my imagination kicked in, and I became creative. George Bernard Shaw said, "Imagination is the beginning of creation."

I begin; well... curiosity told the cat thaaaat...uh, it would be fun to play with the electrical outlet, yeah! And the cat said okay...uh, and then the cat stuck a fork in the outlet, and he was electrocuted. Yeah, Yeah, Yeah, that's what happened...

Each time I would come up with a different story. That's when I realized that imagination is more important than memory.

Memory can **box** you in, **paralyze** you, and keep you from exploring possibilities. Imagination allows you to soar into the unknown, to reach for the impossible. Imagination allows you to find solutions that memory keeps you from finding. We have a problem of living from memory rather than from imagination.

Muhammad Ali, arguably the greatest heavyweight boxer of all time, once said: "The man who has no imagination has no wings. "Humanity has been given a power that no other living creature has, imagination. Through this superpower, humanity has conquered nearly every obstacle that has ever been placed before us. We have been designed to soar above all other creatures on the earth. The Bible states that humanity was given the power to have dominion over all of the works of God's hands (Psalm 8:6). This applies not only to animals and birds but to all obstacles that present themselves between us and becoming our best selves. However, just because you have been given dominion doesn't mean you have dominion. You must seize it, and in order to seize it, you must first see it! We see it in our imagination.

CHAPTER 3

A Personal Triumph of Imagination

"There is the strange power we have of changing facts by the force of the imagination."

—Virginia Woolf

My dad was the most influential man in my life. He had such a brilliant imagination. He was born with a degenerative spinal disease that didn't manifest until he was in his 20s. He and my mother met before it started affecting him. They fell in love and got married. One year after he and my mother married, he had to have surgery for the disease. It left him a quadriplegic. Doctors never expected him to walk or move below his neck again. But my dad could see something no one else could. He would not allow himself to envision being paralyzed for the rest of his life. He had a new wife, a child, and another one on the way. This would not be his future. In his imagination, he could see himself walking. He elected to have the surgery after my youngest sister was born. After surgery, it became a waiting game. Days turned into weeks, weeks turned into months, and months to years. He was still paralyzed. I remember him telling me years later how he would lie in bed and cry because he couldn't scratch his nose. But in his imagination, he could still see himself walking. After three years, he could sit up and soon began walking, first with a walker and then with a cane

I saw my dad accomplish amazing things with his handicap that most men would not try who had a total capacity of their body. The prognosis for his disease was very dim. The average life expectancy was no more than 47 years for someone with my dad's condition, but my dad had an imagination. He couldn't see himself leaving his growing family and leaving his children to be raised by someone else. He passed away in 2019 at the age of 89 and left an incredible legacy for his children, grandchildren, great-grandchildren, and great-great-grandchildren.

One thing my dad would always tell us when we were kids was, "If you don't have what you want, take what you have and make what you want out of it." That's imagination! Often in life, we don't have the things that we want. We don't have the situations that we want. We don't have the opportunities that we want. If we can see what we want in our imagination, we can create what we want from what we have. If your life is not what you want it to be, imagine what you want it to be, use the life you have, and make it what you want.

CHAPTER 4

Catch It Early

"Crazy is the price you pay for having an imagination. It's your superpower. Tapping into the dream. It's a good thing not a bad thing."

—Ruth Ozeki

Warren Buffet stated in his 1998 speech at the University of Florida, "Chains of life are too light to be felt until they are too heavy to be broken." I would add that the chains of our past and memory are too light to be felt until they are too heavy to be broken. When we continually allow past hurts, disappointment, and memory to guide our lives, they become stronger and stronger, slowly dimming our ability to imagine a more extraordinary life, opportunity, and vision.

There is a phrase, "nose blind," that indicates when a person has been around certain smells for so long, they don't smell it anymore. However, everyone else that comes around them can smell it instantly. This is how someone imprisoned by their past memories becomes. They don't realize how the memories of the past constrict their lives, happiness, and outlook. When others notice it and mention it, they become defensive and offended. This is because the pain of the memory has blinded them to the possibilities. They cannot see beyond their prison.

Have you ever noticed how children quickly recover from things? They will play together and then begin to fight one another. Before you know it, they are playing and laughing

again. Even in some of the most traumatic moments of their young lives, after it's over, they are back to being lively without any inhibitions. The mind, heart, and resilience of children are beautiful things. Suppose we could carry the same embodiment of character and resoluteness into adulthood. Can you imagine how different our world would be?

Okay, so we can't go back to our childhood and start over, but we can start today and decide to break out of the prison of our past memories. Change is complicated and sometimes painful because we have to negotiate the wasted time of the past, the brave new world that stands before us, and our own feeling of being weak or gullible for allowing a situation, person, or mindset to keep us in bondage. Regardless of how uncomfortable it may be, becoming free and realizing the possibilities that exist outside the prison necessitate that we change.

Children are allowed to let their imaginations roam free. They become astronauts, cowboys, space explorers, police officers, judges, lawyers, doctors, and anything they can imagine. However, as they get older, they are told to stop daydreaming. They are urged to keep their mind focused on learning what has already been done. Current knowledge is elevated above imagination. The standard has already been set, learn it and memorize it. Children are pushed to follow standardized practices and think in standardized ways, remain stuck in the knowledge of the past, and their imagination is slowly anesthetized.

Children should be encouraged to continue to imagine possibilities. Discoveries that affect your life and the world around you can only be realized and developed through the power of imagination. Imagination requires challenging and questioning the status quo. Just because that's how it has always been done does not mean that that is how it always has to be. Does this mean that, as adults, it is too late? Not at all! Well, what constitutes starting early? If we look at starting early, the most opportune time would be throughout childhood, but I would consider early any time before you close your eyes for the last time. One day free to imagine is worth a lifetime imprisoned to past memories or outdated thinking.

Memory will always stop you short of becoming great, of becoming the best. Memory will always say, **remember** that *you don't have a degree*. You can't achieve it because **remember,** *you were raised in a dysfunctional family*. You will never be financially secure, **remember,** *your family has always been poor*. Your life won't be happy because **remember that** *none of your family members have a happy life*. Memory must be put in its place and controlled, or it will control you.

In contrast, ***imagination*** will say ***I don't care if I've never seen it before,*** in my mind, I can see it happening. ***I don't care if it hasn't been done before...***I can see myself doing it in my imagination... ***I don't care if I've failed many times before...*** I can see myself accomplishing it. It can be done.. In my imagination, I can see it.. If you can see it, you can achieve. Not from memory but from imagination.

CHAPTER 5

To Know or Not to Know

"To know is nothing at all; to imagine is everything."

—Anatole France

Albert Einstein famously said, "Imagination is more important than knowledge. Knowledge is limited. Imagination encircles the world."[1] That statement gives us an idea of how powerful our imagination is. The problem with knowledge is that we often seek it as an end in itself. Knowledge is only as conclusive as the end to which it was stretched. When our goal becomes knowledge alone, it is placed on a pedestal as the absolute. We no longer stretch our minds to further that particular knowledge, and our creativity and imagination become stifled.

Knowledge can become our prison. We should always approach knowledge as a placeholder. It is the understanding of things up until now. With imagination and creativity, that benchmark of knowledge is always moving. Those who stick to previous knowledge without wavering are prisoners to that knowledge. It is pretty egotistical to think that all knowledge in any particular field has been attained. However, some will fight to their final breath if anyone challenges their established metric of knowledge. We often hold to the knowledge we have espoused

---

[1] Albert Einstein, Cosmic religion: With other opinions and aphorisms, Covici-Freide, Publishers, New York, NY, 1931).

to be true like a Pitbull when we should treat knowledge more loosely, knowing that it can change at any time.

Rather than teaching children in school to simply accept the knowledge presented to them, we should encourage them to challenge the knowledge. If it is not correct, or there is a more efficient process, prove it. This will activate the imagination to look not only at the accepted knowledge but also investigate the possibilities of expanding the current understanding. Instead, they are too often discouraged from drawing outside the lines or questioning what has been accepted as fact. This leads to adults who are imagination deficient and will fight for the accepted standard. When we lock ourselves into any particular knowledge, we doom our creativity and imagination. We also relinquish our ability to better ourselves and our environment and move forward for the progression of our world. I will admit that I have found myself often falling into this category. It's how I was raised. Follow the line that is placed before you. Accept the path provided for you, and you'll be fine. Have you heard the phrase "don't rock the boat?" That was probably made up by someone who wanted their view of knowledge to be accepted by everyone. No one's knowledge is irrefutable because the human mind is finite. Each individual in society has a different level of mental capacity, but none is infinite. We would do well to approach knowledge not as an absolute but as a placeholder for more current knowledge to build upon.

CHAPTER 6

Let's Talk Imagination

"Imagination is the only weapon in the war against reality."

—Lewis Carroll

The British Journal of Psychology submits, "Imagination refers to creating mental representations of concepts, ideas, and sensations that are not contemporaneously perceived by the senses."[2] A highly familiar scripture says, "Now faith is the assurance of things hoped for, the conviction of things not seen." (Hebrews 11:1 ESV). Faith is seeing that which cannot be seen with the natural eye. Sounds a lot like imagination. You may not be religious or a person of faith, but I am. I cannot help but associate what the Bible describes as faith with what the world calls imagination. I can't comprehend the imagination that God must have to have created such a beautiful, intelligent, and self-sustaining world. Absolutely awesome!!!

Everything that has been realized, discovered, or brought to light throughout history has been through imagination. Without imagination, we are doomed to exist in iterations of the past. While there is no new thing under the sun, there are things that will not be revealed without imagination. If our imagination is

---

2 Sophie von Stumm and Hannah Scott, "Imagination links with schizotypal beliefs, not with creativity or learning," British Journal of Psychology (2019), 110, 707–726

not strengthened and allowed to flourish, the most valuable discoveries and insights will never be discovered.

Psychotherapist, Social Ecologist, and Corporate trainer Tao de Haas states that "The more you use your imagination, the stronger your 'imagination muscle' will become. You will be pleasantly surprised as you use this ability and tap into this rich source of infinite possibilities."[3] While corporations realize the need for strong creative minds that lead to innovation, our educational systems seem to want to stick to the same old ineffective playbook. Read, study, and learn, but don't draw outside the lines. Stay in the box that has been built for you.

According to history, Albert Einstein is considered one of the most brilliant men ever to live, but he was not necessarily extremely intelligent. However, he was an independent thinker whose imagination propelled him to experiment. Einstein said, "Imagination is everything. It is the preview of life's coming attractions."[4] Wow!! What a fantastic observation. But if this is true, it means we have no view of coming attractions without imagination. I would dare to say there would be no coming attractions at all.

One could say that creation occurs twice. The mind creates the idea, process, or object in your imagination, and then you create it in reality with physical material. The famous painter Vincent Van Gough stated, "I dream my painting, and I paint my dream." Imagination gives us inspiration and animates within us the ability to see beyond. According to *Psychology Today*, research shows that mental practices are almost as effective as

---

[3] Tao de Haas, The Importance Of Imagination, about my brain blog, 18 June 2014 https://www.aboutmybrain.com/blog/the-importance-of-imagination

[4] Albert Einstein, Cosmic religion,: With other opinions and aphorisms, Covici-Freide, Publishers, New York, NY, 1931)

true physical practice in some cases.[5] That's not to say that if I imagine myself doing 150 pushups, that is as good as doing them (oh, how I wish that were the case. I would do a lot more imagining about exercise). The fact is, the same brain patterns are activated when someone physically carries out a task are also activated when the imagination does that same task.

In today's culture, we must train ourselves to unlearn what we have mislearned about how we think. In a memorable quote, Margaret Mead stated, "Children must be taught how to think, not what to think."[6] I believe that many of us today are products of being taught how to think. We find it tough to break out of the box of thought that has been taught to us year after year. What if we stop to imagine a different view of our reality or analyze the knowledge and understanding we have accepted without question? That imagination could possibly lead us to new conclusions, solutions, and reality. Even if it didn't, it has opened up our minds to new possibilities. According to Sylvia Diamiano, founder and CEO of About My Brain Institute, "The more time you spend imagining, the more you are flexing your brain. Learning to tap into this resource can help you think new thoughts, which can translate into results in the office."[7] Continuously recycling old thoughts take us no further than we are in the present, but if we are to progress into the future, we

[5] A.J. Adams, Seeing Is Believing: *The Power of Visualization*, Psychology Today, December 2009.
https://www.psychologytoday.com/us/blog/flourish/200912/seeing-is-believing-the-power-visualization

[6] Margaret Mead, Coming of Age in Samoa, Harper Perennial: New York, NY (2001).

[7] Sylvia Damiano, Your Imagination Is A Powerful Tool - Are You Using It Effectively, 30 January 2020,
https://www.aboutmybrain.com/blog/your-imagination-is-a-powerful-tool-are-you-using-it-effectively

must imagine and think of new thoughts. This is a choice that we must make. Just as our muscles do not want to exercise on their own, the "imagination muscle" doesn't want to move out of the comfort zone of routine, we must train it to do so.

CHAPTER 7

What the World Needs Now

"Imagination is the beginning of creation. You imagine what you desire, you will what you imagine, and at last, you create what you will."

—George Bernard Shaw

I served as a Firefighter/EMT for Dekalb County, GA, for several years. I witnessed horrible automobile accidents and was able to assist when possible. I fought various blazing infernos in Apartment buildings and homes. We were there to assist those who were experiencing emergency conditions. When we could, we would remove them from the dangerous environment. When we could not, we would protect the environment as best we could. However, all of the time, we were not in hazardous environments. As a part of our duties, we were tasked with ensuring that all of the businesses in our territory passed a safety inspection.

Safety inspections were conducted to ensure fire extinguishers and first-aid kits were up to date, fire hoses and sprinkler systems functioned properly, fire exits were lighted, and there were no storage violations that could start or encourage a fire. In many of the newer commercial buildings, you will find a case on the wall. Usually painted red with a glass door. On the door, you see these words "***Break glass in case of emergency.***" Behind the glass, you will find maybe a fire extinguisher, an axe, or a fire hose. All of these things assist in the time of emergency that will not only help you but will help all of those around you. I would like to suggest that the world is in an emergency! Not a fire or an accident. The world is in an imagination emergency. We are slowly but surely losing the superpower of imagination. It is time for the world to recognize that imagination has been placed in a case behind a glass door of past memory, old knowledge, and contentment. We need to break the glass because it is an emergency.

A Global study was done that showed that 75% of people think they are not living up to their creative potential. Why do so many people feel that they are not living up to their creative potential? What has caused them to lose their superpower? Is it possible that our society does not value imagination any longer? Do we not recognize that this great gift, this creative force that we have all been given by our creator, is for the good of all mankind?

In his book, *Understanding the Purpose and Power of Men,* Dr. Myles Monroe writes, "People can go for years without realizing they aren't fulfilling their true purpose. Both individuals and cultures can become comfortable following established roles without questioning their validity."[8] I understand that following the path that has already been established is the easier route to take, but it will also only take you to where everyone else has been. To break new ground and innovate, it will mean taking a route that no one else has taken, exploring what others have not. This takes imagination.

---

[8] Myles Monroe, *Understanding the Purpose and Power of Men,* (New Kensington, PA: Whitaker House, 2001), 15.

The World Economic Forum determined that creativity is among the top three skills workers need beyond 2020. Imagination is the key to innovation, and it must be allowed to grow and mature. Imagination must be nurtured and exercised so that ideas and solutions can find their way out of us. Our educational system must be trained to value and nurture imagination. Our society must embrace the imaginative nature of all of humanity and, rather than stifle it, hone it. Becoming an adult does not mean losing our sense of imagination, to the contrary. As adults, we should master our imagination and let it lead us to greater discoveries, greater realities, and a greater life.

The world is in desperate need of those who want to find and search out new solutions, not those who believe it cannot be done and accept a status quo way of doing business. Innovation involves expanding our minds and the understanding of how to draw on our own and others' ingrained ability to imagine. Recent surveys show that 33% of high school graduates never read another book the rest of their lives, and 42% of college grads never read another book after college. This survey also shows that 70% of US adults have not been in a bookstore in the last five years, and 80% of US families did not buy or read a book last year.[9]

These are sobering statistics. It is easy to see how the power of imagination has dwindled in our society. The passion and fire that once fueled our desire to grow and stretch our minds and imagination have been doused with a deluge of satisfaction after completing high school or college.

---

[9] Michael Kozlowski, "Reading books is on the decline," Goodreader Blog (July 14, 2018), https://goodereader.com/blog/bookselling/reading-books-is-on-the-decline

Our society is in desperate need of solutions for problems, both old and new. We are dealing with challenges that have escaped the understanding and approaches that have been used repeatedly. While many have applied the processes of the past liberally, they often fail miserably. This is not to say that the knowledge and processes of the past are useless, but they do not move us forward from the time in which they were attained. Each period of time should provide fresh new ideas and perspectives that push us forward to achieve more incredible discoveries, inventions, and understanding, but this can only be done through imagination.

Most businesses, organizations, churches, and groups want to grow and develop, but the culture of growth must include the freedom of the people to imagine and be creative. Often this is discouraged at various levels. Some leaders would rather accept mediocrity or sameness than step out of the routine and let the imagination roam. Yes, trying new things is a risk and may end in failure, but everything modern invention ever created was impossible until it wasn't.

According to the About My Brain Institute, "Leaders will need to develop superior skills of innovation requiring imagination and a systemic "seeing" of how all the parts fit together to make a coherent whole."[10] The world needs new ideas, solutions, and inventions to relieve us of the many social and physical ills that plague us daily. There are too many diseases without cures. If we continue to think as we have in the past, we will continue to receive the results we have gotten in the past. When we continue

---

[10] Katharine McLennan, "The Case For the Imagination Age, Building Leaders i4 Neuroleader Model," Edition 1, January 11th, 2016, https://www.aboutmybrain.com/blog/building-leaders-for-the-imagination-age

to use the same processes and programs that have failed up to this point, it indicates that we are more committed to the process or program than we are to the solution.

The Harvard Business Review suggests, "We believe imagination — the capacity to create, evolve, and exploit mental models of things or situations that don't yet exist — is the crucial factor in seizing and creating new opportunities, and finding new paths to growth."[11] When we impede imagination, we cease growth potential. When growth stops, death is imminent. There must be an intentional effort to feed, cultivate, and nurture imagination if our society, businesses, churches, and organizations are to grow and progress.

---

[11] Martin Reeves and Jack Fuller, "We Need Imagination Now More Than Ever," Harvard Business Review Press, April 10, 2020, https://hbr.org/2020/04/we-need-imagination-now-more-than-ever

CHAPTER 8

How Do We Get There

"Imagination is the beginning of creation. You imagine what you desire, you will what you imagine, and at last, you create what you will."

—George Bernard Shaw

The doorway to creativity is imagination. There is no creativity without engaging our imagination. When we engage our imagination, it requires that new neural pathways are created in the brain because your mind is mapping unchartered territory. When the pathways in the brain are already established, the brain, by default will follow the pathways that are established.

Have you driven down a dirt road or a path in the woods? It is rugged and difficult to negotiate, and because the road is not established, you can easily go off course. When I was a young boy, my family moved to Mississippi. My mother was born in Mississippi, and my dad was a country boy from Arkansas. After my dad's battle with his spinal disease, he wanted to move back to the south and to a warmer climate. So, we moved to a rural part of Mississippi because my dad wanted a farm with a garden and animals. We bought a few acres of vacant land and built a farm complete with chickens, pigs, cows, horses, and a garden. The land was overgrown and had to be conditioned for a driveway, the house foundation, as well as paths throughout the property. The driveway and foundation had to be cut with heavy machinery, but the pathways throughout the property were created over time by continually traversing the area.

The point that I am getting to is that the pathways did not exist before my dad imagined where they would be. After the paths were imagined, they had to be traversed over and over before they formed and became established paths. The brain exerts the least amount of energy or activity when accessing memory and pulling information from the known. This is because these are familiar paths of activity for the brain, and connections already exist. But imagination requires new neural connections because the "brain can't rely on connections that have been shaped by past experience."[12]

The brain is similar to our other muscles, it does not want to exert more energy than necessary. Physical trainers will tell you that you need to change up your workout so that you can get the maximum growth and strength of your muscles. The muscles plateau when the same exercises, positions, and form are used exclusively. The tenderness that is felt when you start a new exercise or position is because the muscle is not used to it, but you can't stop, or you'll lose the momentum gained. So, the muscles have to be trained to push past the discomfort in order to gain the desired results. The brain, likewise, would rather follow the established paths of memory and past knowledge than be pushed into the unfamiliar territory of imagination. However, there are practices that we can put into place that will help us to enhance and strengthen our imagination.

---

[12] JANE PORTER, "The Neuroscience of Imagination," FASTCO WORKS

Here are a few things that we can do to strengthen and build our imagination:

- **Challenge Your Existing Perceptions** – What we see is often derived more from our memory than from our eyes. Research estimates that 80% of visual perception is from memory, and only 20% is actually input through the eyes.[13] Evaluate how much of what you perceive is from memory and train yourself to perceive it differently.

- **Daydream** – this is something that is often discouraged as we get older. We fill our days, hours, and minutes with work, media, and interacting with others and often set aside no time to open our minds to imagine, to think of possibilities that do not currently exist. Set aside time daily to expand your imagination, to open your mind to the unseen, the possibilities, and the potential of a better world.

- **Use your voice-** Find places where you can discuss your ideas and thoughts without fear of judgment. It may even mean talking to yourself. Vocalization is known to tap into our emotions which can engage the imagination.

- **Ask More Questions** – We often accept stated facts without question, depending on who it comes from. We usually don't question ourselves concerning our habits or why we follow certain routines. When we ask questions, it forces us to ponder our actions and reasonings as well as those of others.

- **Find Your Place of Solace** – Find a place where you can go to free your mind of daily problems and stress. It could

---

[13] Richard Gregory, 'Brainy Mind', British Medical Journal, 19 December 1998, issue 317: pp. 1693–1695

be simply sitting outside looking at the stars with a cup of coffee or going and sitting in the park. These types of times can stimulate the imagination.

These exercises are by no means exhaustive of the ways that you can stimulate the imagination, but this is a good place to start.

CHAPTER 9

It's Time to Remember

Imagination is the voice of daring. If there is anything godlike about God, it is that. He dared to imagine everything.

—Henry Miller

I am unapologetically a man of faith, and I believe that all of humanity was created in the image of God, our creator. The Bible states that "then the LORD God formed the man of dust from the ground and breathed into his nostrils the breath of life, and the man became a living creature" (Gen 2:7 ESV). When God breathed into humanity, the essence of who God is was placed within us. God is a God of imagination. The universe was created from nothing, and through God's imagination and His Word, it came into existence. We are endowed with imaginative power from God that allows us to see the invisible, conceive the impossible, and believe the incredible. That being said, humans can quickly forget all that they are capable of accomplishing. Incredible feats that were once thought to be impossible have been achieved by ordinary human beings who have an extraordinary imagination.

We must remember who we are and what we are capable of achieving. The knowledge of self is often suppressed by the cares, stress, and daily routines of life. We become so focused on taking care of family, paying bills, trying to get that promotion, or maintaining that GPA that we forget the power that we have in our imagination. We must relinquish those cares if we are to allow our superpower to rise to the top. We will always have a care in this world, but we must never allow the concerns to crowd out the power that illuminates the dark places and reveals the solutions to problems that are otherwise unknown.

Susan West, founder of TheLeadershipResource.com suggests that the imagination of most adults has been suppressed. She states, "We must learn to uncover it again. At birth, we had 100% imagination, it has been said that we have only 4% usage of imagination by age 7. Studies as referenced in Success at Life, "show remarkably, even shockingly, that in the first five years of life we as children are told no over fifty thousand times and yes only five thousand times."[14]

It is evident that we are often our own worst enemies when it comes to imagination. The culture must change and become one that welcomes diversity in thought and ideas that conflict with those of the past. Parents must become encouragers of their children's imagination even as they get older. As adults, we must change the culture to one of openness and acceptance where sharing of ideas, both traditional and nontraditional, must are encouraged and celebrated.

In the Scriptures, we find several time where Jesus admonishes the disciples to be more like children. I would suggest that Jesus recognized the honesty, love, and imagination in children that adults seem to lose all too quickly. "Imagination invites us to breathe, to dream, and to be fully present to the

---

[14] Susan West, Engaging Your Imagination, The Leadership Resource, Leadership Development skills (MAY 20, 2011), http://theleadershipresource.com/engaging-your-imagination

wonder of it all."[15] To view the world with the splendor and amazement of a child can reactivate the imagination that the world so urgently needs.

---

[15] KAYTI CHRISTIAN, How To Engage Your Imagination As A Spiritual Practice, The Good Trade, APR 7, 2021 www.thegoodtrade.com/features/imagination-spiritual-practice.

CHAPTER 10

It's In Your Hands, Now What

"There is no doubt that creativity is the most important human resource of all. Without creativity, there would be no progress, and we would be forever repeating the same patterns."

—Edward de Bono

I enjoy watching movies and often try to figure out the plot beforehand, but in recent years I have noticed that there is a lack of creativity. There are so many movies that are simply remakes of older movies. It seems that the same reality exists in the scientific, business, religious, and technological environments. Is it laziness, lack of desire to push harder, stretch further, or is it that we have simply lost the desire to engage our imagination? If our society resolves that this is the reality that we can live with, then we are always doomed to be less than our potential can provide.

Jim Loree, C.E.O. of Stanley Black & Decker states, "Never in our lifetimes has the power of imagination been more important in defining our immediate future....Leaders need to seize the opportunity to inspire and harness the imagination of their organizations during this challenging time."[16] As I stated earlier, we are in an emergency. Not just because of Covid, but because of all of the other diseases that have yet to arise. We are in an

---

[16] Jim Loree, "WHAT WILL COVID-19 CHANGE," Rob Hoskins In the News, May 11, 2022, https://robhoskins.onehope.net/category/in-the-news/

emergency because of the prisons of hate, discouragement, and low self-esteem. We are in an emergency because we are allowing our most potent weapon, our superpower, to dissipate. It's time to break the glass of memory, of the past, of fear, and pull out our imagination so we can conquer the problems and difficulties that lie before us.

I have developed an acronym to suggest the steps to break out of our respective prisons and reactivate our imagination. The acronym is EMPTY.

E- you must **evaluate** your belief, knowledge, and memories.

- Are they keeping you stuck and not allowing you to move forward? If they keep you stuck, it's a prison. Get rid of it!

- Do they give you the sense of feeling complete or finished? If they make you feel complete or finished, it's a prison. Beliefs, knowledge, and memories should push you forward to grow and do better, not make you feel finished.

M- make a list of why these beliefs, knowledge, and memories do or do not benefit your future growth.

P- place priority on the unknown and unseen.

- What is it that I have not considered that could possibly increase my potential?

- What is it that I don't see that could increase my potential?

- What has no one else done to solve this problem?

T- take steps to break the bonds of memory, knowledge, and the past that do not serve to reveal your best self.

Y- You!! Give yourself permission to imagine the improbable and impossible.

If you take these steps and consistently implement them, over time, you will find yourself becoming free to soar in your imagination. You will come to recognize solutions that you have not seen before. Your outlook will become more promising and optimistic. The things that once restricted your progress will no longer have a hold over you.

Conclusion

I leave you with this one last word, your imagination is not dead. It may be dormant, or smothered under loads of memories, knowledge, and accepted roles or statuses. You can reactivate your imagination and thereby reactivate your ability to see and create the future solutions and answers that this world needs. The growth, development, and progress of your business, organization, church, and our world hangs in the balance of how we use, strengthen, or ignore the power of our imagination. Will we continue to run on the hamster wheel of life because we feel that where we are and what we have achieved We must come to the realization that life is a journey not a destination. Life should be always progressing and moving forward. When we have reached the place where we feel it is time to stop progressing that is the time we should plan to die. Life is progress and growth and there is no progress without imagination. Break out of the prison of past knowledge and memories. Develop your imagination. Soar to new levels of innovation. You will find that when you open that door the possibilities are limitless.

References

Albert Einstein, Cosmic religion, With other opinions and aphorisms, Covici-Freide, Publishers, New York, NY, 1931)

A.J. Adams, Seeing Is Believing: *The Power of Visualization*, Psychology Today, December 2009.

https://www.psychologytoday.com/us/blog/flourish/200912/seeing-is-believing-the-power-visualization

Jane Porter, "The Neuroscience of Imagination," FASTCO WORKS

Katharine McLennan, "The Case For the Imagination Age, Building Leaders i4 Neuroleader Model," Edition 1, January 11th, 2016, https://www.aboutmybrain.com/blog/building-leaders-for-the-imagination-age

Kayti Christian, How To Engage Your Imagination As A Spiritual Practice, The Good Trade, APR 7, 2021 ww.thegoodtrade.com/features/imagination-spiritual-practice.

Margaret Mead, Coming of Age in Samoa, Harper Perennial: New York, NY (2001).

Martin Reeves and Jack Fuller, "We Need Imagination Now More Than Ever," Harvard Business Review Press, April 10, 2020, https://hbr.org/2020/04/we-need-imagination-now-more-than-ever

Michael Kozlowski, "Reading books is on the decline," Goodreader Blog (July 14, 2018), https://goodereader.com/blog/bookselling/reading-books-is-on-the-decline

Myles Monroe, *Understanding the Purpose and Power of Men,*(New Kensington, PA: Whitaker House, 2001), 15.

Richard Gregory, 'Brainy Mind', British Medical Journal, 19 December 1998, issue 317: pp. 1693–1695

Sophie von Stumm and Hannah Scott, "Imagination links with schizotypal beliefs, not with creativity or learning," British Journal of Psychology (2019), 110, 707–726

Susan West, Engaging Your Imagination, The Leadership Resource, Leadership Development skills (MAY 20, 2011), http://theleadershipresource.com/engaging-your-imagination

Sylvia Damiano, Your Imagination Is A Powerful Tool - Are You Using It Effectively, 30 January 2020,

https://www.aboutmybrain.com/blog/your-imagination-is-a-powerful-tool-are-you-using-it-effectively

Tao de Haas, The Importance Of Imagination, about my brain blog, 18 June 2014 https://www.aboutmybrain.com/blog/the-importance-of-imagination

15796384R00024